i SPY
WITH MY LITTLE EYE...
EASTER!

READY? LET'S BEGIN!

LET'S CONNECT:

🌎 : PamparamKidsBooks.com

▶ : Pamparam Kids Books

📌 : Pamparam Kids Books

📷 : @PamparamKidsBooks

i SPY WITH MY LITTLE EYE, SOMETHING GREEN:

THE EGG

is GREEN!

i SPY WITH MY LITTLE EYE, SOMETHING BEGINNING WITH...

B

i SPY WITH MY LITTLE EYE, SOMETHING SWEET:

THE MUFFIN

is SWEET!

I SPY WITH MY LITTLE EYE, SOMETHING BEGINNING WITH...

F

i SPY WITH MY LITTLE EYE, SOMETHING BROWN:

THE RABBIT

is BROWN!

I SPY WITH MY LITTLE EYE, SOMETHING BEGINNING WITH...

i SPY WITH MY LITTLE EYE, SOMETHING ROUND:

THE COOKIE

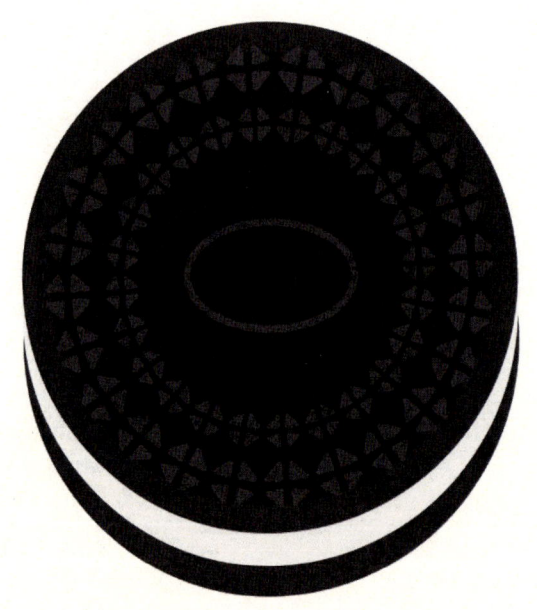

is ROUND!

I SPY WITH MY LITTLE EYE, SOMETHING BEGINNING WITH...

M

ONSTER!

I SPY WITH MY LITTLE EYE, SOMETHING YELLOW:

THE CHICK

is YELLOW!

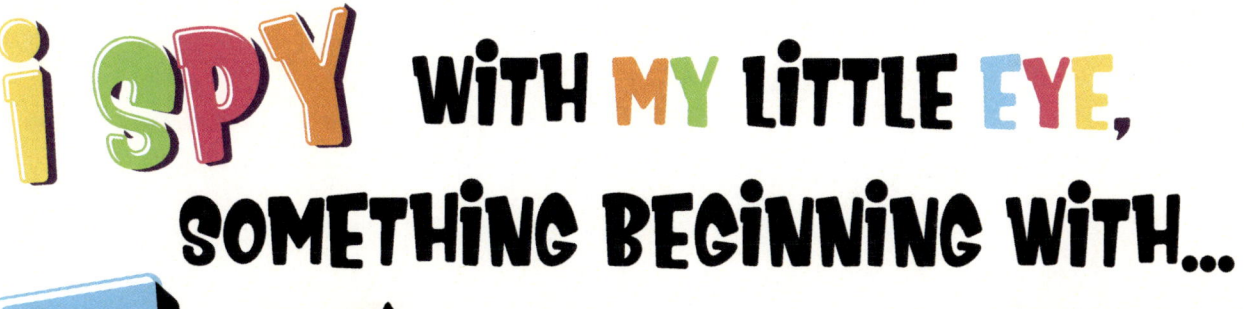

i SPY WITH MY LITTLE EYE, SOMETHING BEGINNING WITH...

E

I SPY WITH MY LITTLE EYE, SOMETHING WITH BIG EARS:

THE BUNNY

HAS BIG EARS!

i SPY WITH MY LITTLE EYE, SOMETHING BEGINNING WITH...

J

J ELLY BEANS!

i SPY WITH MY LITTLE EYE, SOMETHING BLUE:

THE BUTTERFLY

is BLUE!

i SPY WITH MY LITTLE EYE, SOMETHING BEGINNING WITH...

I SPY WITH MY LITTLE EYE, SOMETHING YOU SEE IN SPRING:

YOU CAN SEE A CHICK COMING OUT OF AN EGG

IN SPRING!

i SPY WITH MY LITTLE EYE, SOMETHING BEGINNING WITH...

I SPY WITH MY LITTLE EYE, SOMETHING PURPLE:

THE HEART

is PURPLE!

I SPY WITH MY LITTLE EYE, SOMETHING BEGINNING WITH...

P

I SPY WITH MY LITTLE EYE, SOMETHING THAT FLIES:

THE BEE

FLiES!

Made in the USA
Middletown, DE
03 April 2020